My Allah Series

BE THANKFUL TO ALLAH

Kisa Kids Publications

AL-KISA FOUNDATION
WWW.KISAKIDS.ORG

PARENTS' CORNER

وَاشْكُرُوا لِي وَلَا تَكْفُرُونِ

And thank Me and do not be ungrateful to Me
(Sūrat al-Baqarah, Verse 152)

Dear Parents/Guardians,

Gratefulness is a fundamental concept in Islāmic Akhlāq. To possess true shukr and gratefulness means to use Allāh's blessings wisely and for their true purpose: submission and nearness to Allāh. Unfortunately, gratefulness is a characteristic that has all but lost its intrinsic value in today's society.

Allāh says in the Qurʾān, *"And He has given you all that you had asked Him. If you count Allāh's blessings, you will not be able to count them. Indeed man is most unfair and ungrateful!"* (14:34)

Imām ʿAlī (A) has said, "The minimum responsibility we have towards Allāh is not to use His blessings in the path of disobedience."

In the Qurʾān, we are urged to try and attain the status of the shākirīn, those who are grateful. As parents, it is very important that we teach our children to be grateful at all levels: in our hearts, speech, and actions. We can do this by recognizing that all blessings are from Allāh, verbally expressing gratitude, and using our blessings in their intended manner. Through this book, inshāAllāh your children will discover some of the ways we can be grateful!

With Duʿas,
Kisa Kids Publications

There are many ways to thank the people who help us everyday.
We thank our parents by giving them kisses and listening to what they say.

What are some things you can thank your parents for?

We thank our teachers by giving them gifts,
and we love to watch as their smiles begin to lift.

What do you thank your teacher for?

How can we thank Allah when He has given us so much?
He has given us family, friends, and food that we eat for dinner and lunch.

What do you see in the picture that the family should thank Allah for?

Allah gave us hands, legs, and eyes so we can play on the swings. We should thank Allah when we use any of these things.

How do you use your hands, legs, and eyes when you are at the park?

7

Allah has given us delicious foods, including fruits and yummy veggies. How can we thank Allah when we eat all of these goodies?

What is your favorite food that you are thankful to Allah for?

8

We can thank Allah by using gentle words and doing good deeds.
I am thanking Allah by kindly helping my sister with what she needs.

What good things have you done?

9

When we help our mother water the plants, we are thanking Allah for our wonderful hands.

How do you use your hands to help your mother?

10

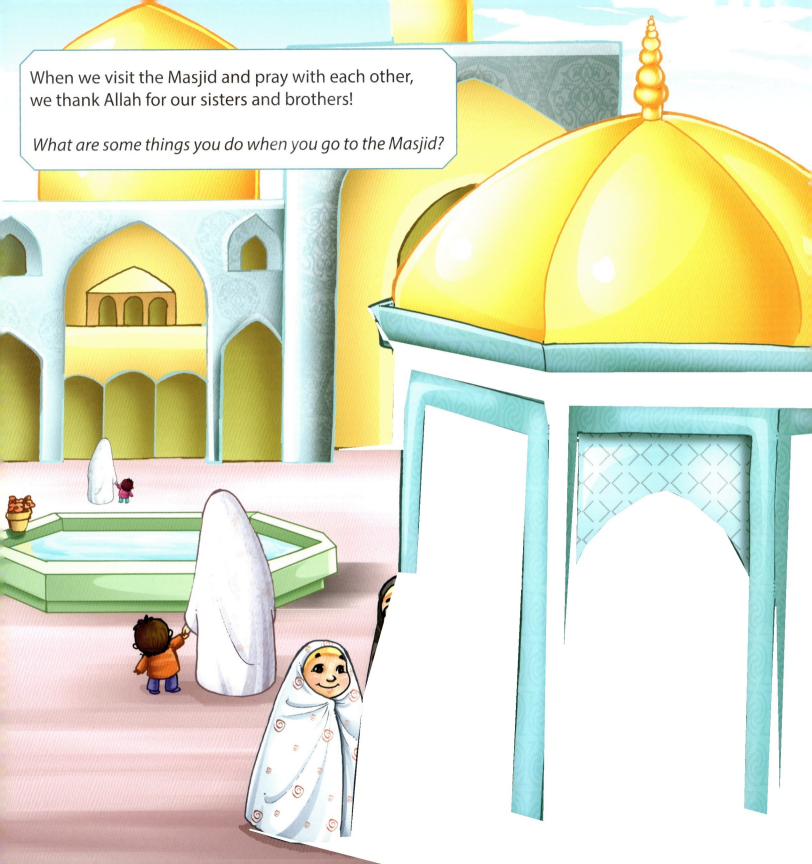

When we visit the Masjid and pray with each other, we thank Allah for our sisters and brothers!

What are some things you do when you go to the Masjid?

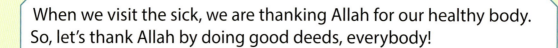

When we visit the sick, we are thanking Allah for our healthy body. So, let's thank Allah by doing good deeds, everybody!

Let's practice saying, "Thank you, Allah!"
"Shukran lillaah!"